History of Islam

Life of Prophet Adam (Alayhis Salaam)

Life of Prophet Nooh (Alayhis Salaam)

Life of Prophet Ayyoob (Alayhis Salaam)

Life of Prophet Muhammad (Sallallahu Alayhis Salaam)

Islamic Learning Books – Grade 1 of 6

Published By : Islamic Book Store

Prepared by:
Jamiatul Ulama (KZN)
Ta'limi Board
4 Third Avenue
P.O.Box 26024
Isipingo Beach
4115
South Africa

Published by:
Islamic Book Store
302 Saad Residancy
Sahin Park M G Road
Bardoli Surat Gujarat
India 394601
UDYAM REGISTRATION NUMBER :
UDYAM-GJ-22-0457400

Table of Contents

Introduction to History i

Hadhrat Aadam (alayhis salaam) 1
Lesson 1 1
Lesson 2 3
Lesson 3 5
Lesson 4 7
Lesson 5 9
Lessons learnt from the life of Hadhrat Aadam (alayhis salaam) 11

Hadhrat Nooh (alayhis salaam) 13
Lesson 6 13
Lesson 7 15
Lesson 8 17
Lesson 9 19
Lessons learnt from the life of Hadhrat Nooh (alayhis salaam) 21

Hadhrat Ayyoob (alayhis salaam) 22
Lesson 10 22
Lesson 11 24
Lesson 12 26
Lessons learnt from the life of Hadhrat Ayyoob (alayhis salaam) 28

Nabi Muhammad (sallallahu alayhi wasallam) 29
Lesson 13 29
Lesson 14 31
Lesson 15 33
Lesson 16 35
Lesson 17 37

$$\bismillah$$

Introduction to Islamic History

The Qur-aan Shareef discusses many incidents of past nations in great length. The reason for mentioning these incidents is so that we may take a lesson from them; to stay away from those things that brought ruin to them as well as implement and apply those aspects that made them successful. Many stories of the Ambiyaa (alayhimus salaam) are discussed in detail in the Qur-aan Shareef to strengthen our hearts.

History has always been one of the key tools for any nation reaching the peaks of success.

This subject, if taught correctly, can become the most enjoyable subject for any child. On the contrary, if it is just read out without properly explaining the events and the lessons behind each event, it can also become the most boring and difficult subject for a learner.

Stories of some of the Ambiyaa (alayhimus salaam) are discussed in this book and each story has great lessons for us to learn.

Teachers should try their best to be real, alive and vivid when teaching this subject to make the lesson as enjoyable as possible for the learners.

May Allah Ta'ala accept our broken efforts for His Deen and crown them with success. Aameen.

Ta'limi Board (KZN)

Safar 1445

LESSON 1

HADHRAT AADAM
(alayhis salaam)

mountain	sun	moon
sky	sea	rivers
trees	sand	names

- Allah Ta'ala made the **sky**, the **sun** and the **moon**.
- Allah Ta'ala made the **trees** and the **mountains**.
- Allah Ta'ala made the **seas** and the **rivers**.
- Allah Ta'ala made all the **people** in this **world**.
- The **first** person Allah Ta'ala made was **Hadhrat Aadam (alayhis salaam)**.
- Allah Ta'ala made Hadhrat Aadam (alayhis salaam) from **sand**.
- Allah Ta'ala taught Hadhrat Aadam (alayhis salaam) the **names** of all the **things** in this **world** and what they are used for.

COLOUR IN THE PICTURES

LESSON 2

HADHRAT AADAM
(alayhis salaam)

angels	light	jinn
fire	sajdah	angry
shaytaan	pride	better

- After Allah Ta'ala created Hadhrat Aadam (alayhis salaam), He told the **angels** to make **sajdah** to him.
- Allah Ta'ala had created the **angels** and **jinn** before Hadhrat Aadam (alayhis salaam).
- Allah Ta'ala made the **angels** from **light**.
- Allah Ta'ala made the **jinn** from **fire**.
- Hadhrat Aadam (alayhis salaam) was made from **sand**.
- All the angels and jinn made sajdah to Hadhrat Aadam (alayhis salaam) **except Shaytaan**.
- Shaytaan did not want to make **sajdah** to Hadhrat Aadam (alayhis salaam) because he was made from **fire** and Hadhrat Aadam (alayhis salaam) was made from **sand**.
- He felt that he was **better** than Hadhrat Aadam (alayhis salaam). He had too much of **pride**.
- **Shaytaan** was disobedient to Allah Ta'ala.
- Allah Ta'ala became **very angry** with Shaytaan.

JOIN THE DOTS

Aadam

LESSON 3
HADHRAT AADAM
(alayhis salaam)

Jannah	gardens	fruit
gold	silver	jewels
lonely	wife	Hawwa

- Allah Ta'ala then gave Hadhrat Aadam (alayhis salaam) a **beautiful home** in **Jannah**.
- Jannah is a **beautiful place** full of **gardens**, **rivers** and **fruit trees**.
- The houses in Jannah are not made out of bricks and stones like the houses we live in. It is made with **gold, silver** and **jewels**.
- Hadhrat Aadam (alayhis salaam) was **living alone** in Jannah.
- He was **feeling lonely** and **wished** for someone to live with him.
- Allah Ta'ala then made **Hawwa (radhiyallahu anha)**.
- She was the **first lady** that Allah Ta'ala created.
- Allah Ta'ala made her **a wife for Hadhrat Aadam (alayhis salaam)** so he will not be lonely.
- Hadhrat Aadam (alayhis salaam) and Hawwa (radhiyallahu anha) **lived happily** in **Jannah**.

JOIN THE WORDS

The First Lady — A beautiful place full of gardens, rivers and fruit trees

Angels — Made from gold and silver

Jannah — Hawwa (Radhiyallahu Anha)

The houses in Jannah — Created from light

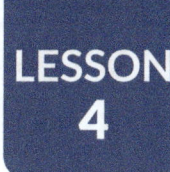

trees	tricked	enjoy
clothes	disappeared	mistake
forgive	jealous	delicious

- In Jannah Allah Ta'ala placed lots of **trees** with **delicious fruit**.
- Allah Ta'ala told Hadhrat Aadam (alayhis salaam) and Hawwa (radhiyallahu anha) to **eat and enjoy the fruits**.
- But there was **one tree** which Allah Ta'ala told them **NOT to eat** from.
- **Shaytaan** was **jealous** of Hadhrat Aadam (alayhis salaam) because Allah Ta'ala loved Hadhrat Aadam (alayhis salaam) and made him live in Jannah.
- To be **jealous** means you **are NOT happy to see** someone enjoying something special.
- **Shaytaan** wanted Hadhrat Aadam (alayhis salaam) and Hawwa (radhiyallahu anha) to be **taken out of Jannah**.
- He thought of a plan that will make them **lose** their **beautiful home in Jannah**.
- One day **Shaytaan tricked** Hadhrat Aadam (alayhis salaam) and Hawwa (radhiyallahu anha) to eat from this tree which Allah Ta'ala asked them not to eat from.
- He told them that if they eat from that tree, they will live in **Jannah forever**.

- Hadhrat Aadam (alayhis salaam) and Hawwa (radhiyallahu anha) **mistakenly ate** from that tree.
- When they ate from that tree, their **clothes disappeared** from their **bodies**.
- Hadhrat Aadam (alayhis salaam) and Hawwa (radhiyallahu anha) **realised** that they **made a mistake** by eating from this tree.
- They **cried** and asked Allah Ta'ala to **forgive** them.

SPOT THE 5 DIFFERENCES

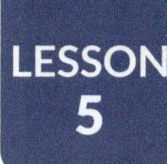

LESSON 5

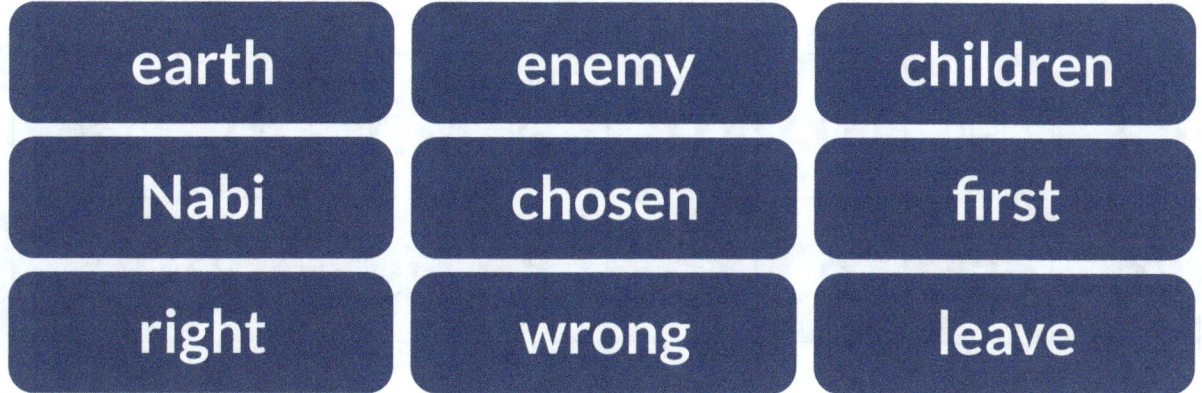

- Allah Ta'ala forgave Hadhrat Aadam (alayhis salaam) and Hawwa (radhiyallahu anha) but told them that they have to **leave Jannah**.
- Allah Ta'ala sent Hadhrat Aadam (alayhis salaam) and Hawwa (radhiyallahu anha) to **live** on **earth**.
- The **earth** is this **world** we are all **living in**.
- **Shaytaan** was also sent to live on earth, because he **disobeyed** Allah Ta'ala.
- **Shaytaan** was the **enemy** of Hadhrat Aadam (alayhis salaam) and Hawwa (radhiyallahu anha).
- Hadhrat Aadam (alayhis salaam) and Hawwa (radhiyallahu anha) had **many children** who lived with them.
- We are all from the **children** of **Hadhrat Aadam (alayhis salaam)** and **Hawwa (radhiyallahu anha)** and they are our **great, great, great** grandparents.
- Allah Ta'ala made Hadhrat Aadam (alayhis salaam) **the first Nabi** on **earth**.
- A **Nabi** is a man **chosen** by Allah Ta'ala who teaches people what is **right** and **wrong**.

- Hadhrat Aadam (alayhis salaam) **taught** his **children** what was **good** and what was **bad**.

WORD SEARCH

FIND THE FOLLOWING WORDS
aadam | jannah | shaytaan | earth | prophet | hawwa

j	a	n	n	a	h	b	a
c	s	e	o	r	s	h	a
h	e	a	k	p	s	h	d
a	b	e	a	r	t	h	a
w	j	k	o	o	t	h	m
w	l	w	p	p	l	n	h
a	j	k	h	h	t	s	m
d	f	k	e	e	r	t	h
s	h	a	y	t	a	a	n

Lessons from the life of Hadhrat Aadam *(alayhis salaam)*

- We must worship Allah Ta'ala because He is our Creator.
- Allah Ta'ala made Hadhrat Aadam (alayhis salaam) and we are all the children of Hadhrat Aadam (alayhis salaam).
- Shaytaan is our enemy and he wants us to do all the wrong things.
- If we make a mistake or a sin, then we must ask Allah Ta'ala to forgive us.
- We must not have pride and think that we are better than anyone.
- We must not be jealous of anyone.

COLOUR IN THE PICTURE BELOW

LESSON 6
HADHRAT NOOH
(alayhis salaam)

passed away	good	shaytaan
Jahannam	jealous	statue
idol	plan	help

- After many **years**, Hadhrat Aadam (alayhis salaam) **passed away**.
- The **children** of Hadhrat Aadam (alayhis salaam) were **still living** in this world.
- They were **good people** and **worshipped Allah Ta'ala alone**.
- **Shaytaan** became **jealous** of them.
- He **did not** want them to **be good** people and go to **Jannah**.
- He **wanted** them to make **Allah angry** and then Allah will send them to **Jahannam**.
- **Shaytaan** thought of **a plan**.
- He made the people think of their **family** who **passed away**.
- Then he told them, "Why don't you make a **picture**/ **statue** of that person so you don't **forget** them."
- The people **thought** that this was a good idea, so they began making pictures/ statues of their **family** who **passed away**.
- Then, every time they had **a problem**, they would go to the **statue** for help.
- This **statue** is called an **Idol**.

13

- They started making dua to the idol instead of **making dua** to **Allah Ta'ala**.
- Slowly the people stopped **worshipping Allah** Ta'ala and began worshipping these idols.
- Shaytaan was **very happy**. His plan **worked** very well.

JOIN THE DOTS

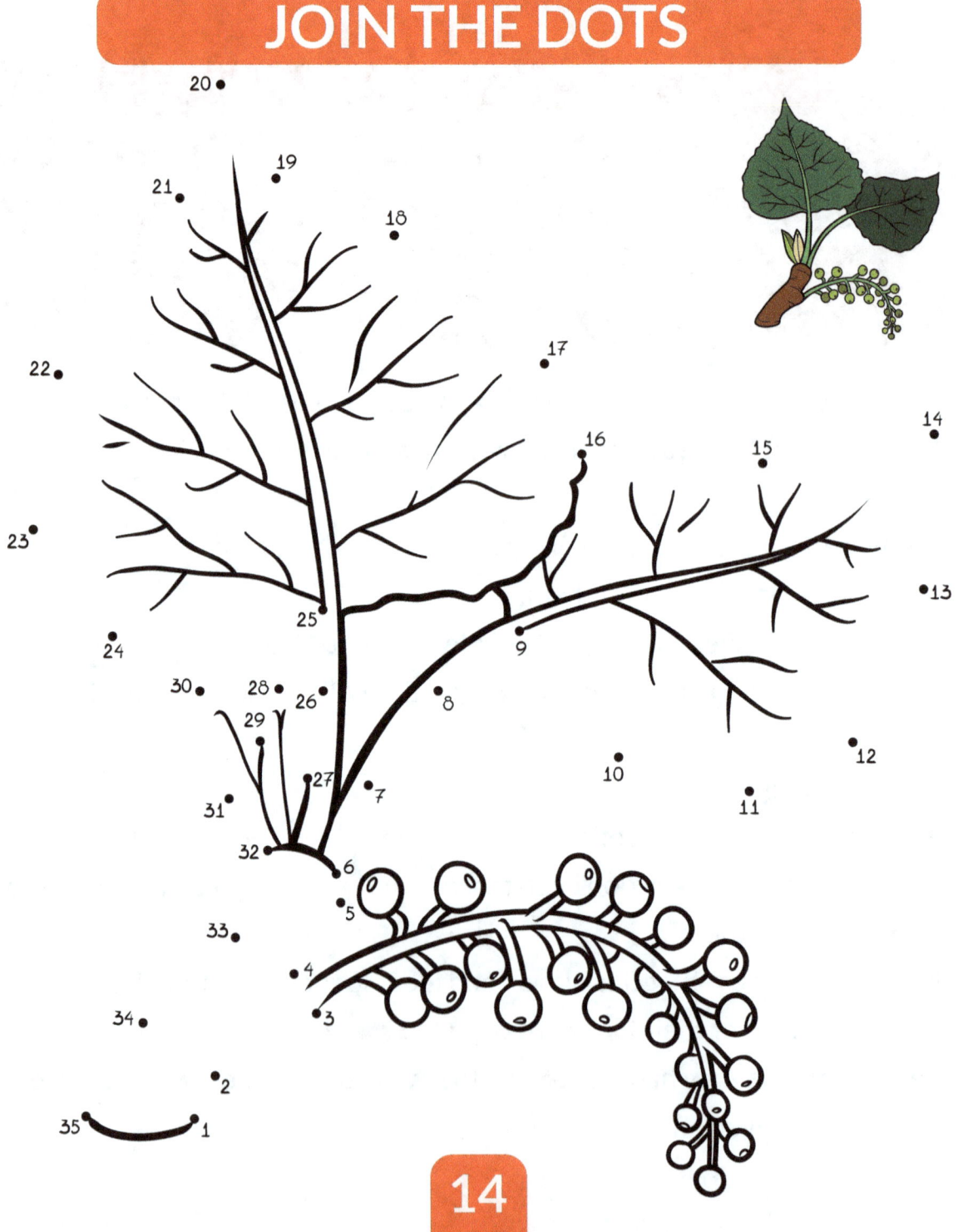

LESSON 7: HADHRAT NOOH (alayhis salaam)

idols	guide	prophet
teach	950	82
poor	listen	worship

- The people had stopped worshipping Allah Ta'ala. They were doing a **very bad** thing. They were **worshipping idols**.
- So, Allah Ta'ala **sent a man** to guide the people and teach them **NOT** to worship idols.
- His name was **Hadhrat Nooh (alayhis salaam)**.
- Allah Ta'ala made him **a Nabi** to **guide** the people.
- Hadhrat Nooh (alayhis salaam) explained to **the people** that what they **were doing was wrong**.
- He told them to **leave out** worshipping the idols and go back to **worshipping Allah Ta'ala**.
- But the people **did not** want to **listen**.
- Hadhrat Nooh (alayhis salaam) **did not give up**.
- He kept on calling the people to worship Allah Ta'ala for **950 years**.
- Only **82 people accepted** his message and **started worshipping Allah Ta'ala**.
- These were the **poor** and **humble people**.
- The rest of the **people did not listen** to him and carried on worshipping idols.

CROSS WORD PUZZLE

			I						
			D				M		
P				P	H				T
							S		
			S				S		
							G		
P	E	O					E		

16

LESSON 8

HADHRAT NOOH
(alayhis salaam)

- proud
- warned
- angry
- ark
- made fun
- liar
- animal
- male
- female

- Only the **poor** and **humble** people listened to Hadhrat Nooh (alayhis salaam).
- The **rich** and **proud** people called Hadhrat Nooh (alayhis salaam) a **liar** and carried on worshipping idols.
- Hadhrat Nooh (alayhis salaam) **warned** them that if they do not listen, Allah Ta'ala will become **angry** with them and **punish them**.
- **They did not care** and told Hadhrat Nooh (alayhis salaam) to send the **punishment** of Allah Ta'ala on them if he was a true prophet.
- After calling his people to Allah Ta'ala for **950 years**, most of his people still did not listen.
- Hadhrat Nooh (alayhis salaam) asked Allah Ta'ala to **punish them**.
- Allah Ta'ala commanded Hadhrat Nooh (alayhis salaam) to build a **big ship** called an **Ark**.
- The people **made fun** of Hadhrat Nooh (alayhis salaam) and **laughed at him** as he was building a ship on **dry land**. There was **no water around**.
- After the ship was built, Allah Ta'ala told Hadhrat Nooh (alayhis salaam) to put all the **good people** who believed in Allah Ta'ala in the ship.

- Then Allah Ta'ala told him to put a **male** and **female** i.e. mother and father of every animal into the Ark.
- For example, a **rooster** and a **hen**, a **bull** and a **cow**, a **lion** and a **lioness**.
- The Ark was now full of the **good people** and all the **different animals**.

HELP THE ANIMALS ONTO THE ARK

ARK

LESSON 9

HADHRAT NOOH
(alayhis salaam)

punishment	water	drowned
flood	safe	world
son	sailed	sky

- Allah Ta'ala then sent down his **punishment** on the people.
- He sent a **great flood**.
- Water came pouring down from the **sky** and gushing from under the **earth**.
- The whole **world** was **drowned** in **water**.
- Only Hadhrat Nooh (alayhis salaam) and those on the **Ark were safe**.
- The **Ark sailed** on top of the **water**.
- Hadhrat Nooh's (alayhis salaam) own **son** and **wife** did **not** listen to him.
- They did not come into the Ark and so they also **drowned** in the flood.
- Only those who **believed** in Allah Ta'ala were **saved**.

HELP THE ARK MAKE ITS WAY TO THE MOUNTAIN

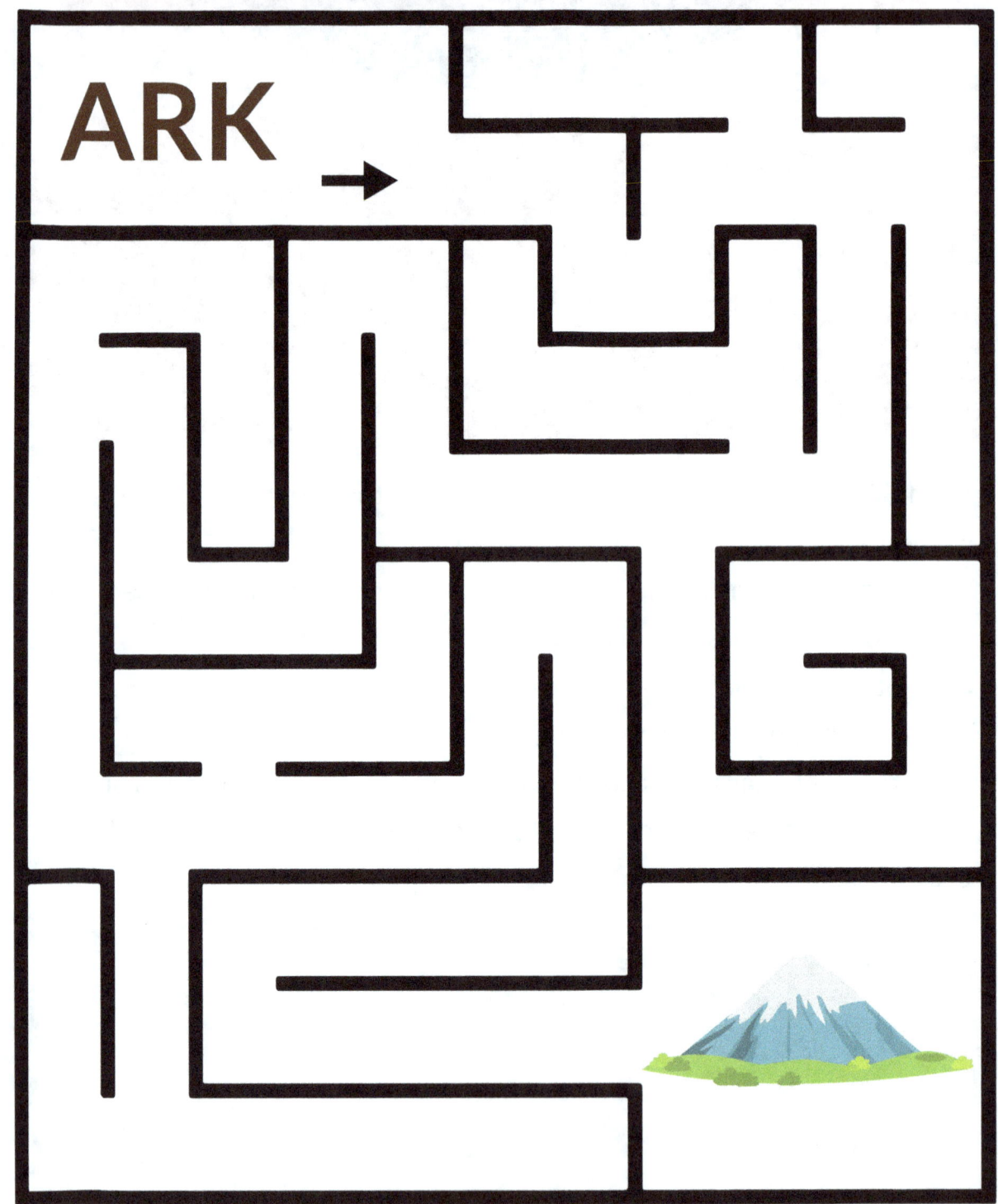

Lessons from the life of Hadhrat Nooh (alayhis salaam)

- Do not worship anything or anyone besides Allah Ta'ala.
- We must not make pictures or statues of anyone. For example, we must not take photographs of people, paint or draw pictures of people or animals. This will lead us to doing wrong and it makes Allah Ta'ala angry.
- Always listen to someone who is teaching us good like our Apa or Moulana in Madrasah.
- Do not laugh or make fun of your Apa, Moulana, any pious people and the Prophets.
- Be friends with good people. Do not be friends with people who make you do wrong things.
- We must not do anything that makes Allah Ta'ala angry such as fighting, lying, etc.
- If Allah Ta'ala is angry and punishes you, no one can save you. Remember Hadhrat Nooh's (alayhis salaam) son was drowned even though he was the son of a Nabi.
- Always try and be with those people who are poor and humble. Allah Ta'ala loves the poor people

LESSON 10
HADHRAT AYYOOB
(alayhis salaam)

generous	strong	family
Rahmah	fourteen	healthy
poor	respected	land

- Allah Ta'ala sent **many prophets** to teach the people what is right and what is wrong.
- One of the prophets that Allah Ta'ala sent was **Hadhrat Ayyoob (alayhis salaam)**.
- Allah Ta'ala blessed Hadhrat Ayyoob (alayhis salaam) with a **lot of land**, **animals** and **money**.
- Hadhrat Ayyoob (alayhis salaam) was a **kind** and **generous** person.
- He would **share** his **money** with the **poor people**.
- He was also blessed with a **lovely family**.
- He had a wife named **Rahmah** and **fourteen beautiful children**.
- He was a **strong** and **healthy man**.
- Everyone **respected** and **loved** Hadhrat Ayyoob (alayhis salaam).

COLOUR IN THE TREASURE BOX

LESSON 11

HADHRAT AYYOOB
(alayhis salaam)

test	money	took away
health	sick	complain
patient	remembered	sabr

- One day Allah Ta'ala decided to **test** Hadhrat Ayyoob (alayhis salaam).
- First Allah Ta'ala **took away** all his **land**, **animals** and **money**.
- He **became very poor**.
- Then Allah Ta'ala **took away all his children**.
- They all passed away and he was **left alone** with his wife.
- Then Allah Ta'ala **took away** his **health**.
- He **became very sick**.
- But Hadhrat Ayyoob (alayhis salaam) **did not complain**.
- He **did not** complain when he lost his money.
- He **did not** complain when he lost his children.
- He **did not** complain when he lost his health.
- He was **patient** and made **sabr**.
- He **still remembered** Allah Ta'ala and continued to **worship** Allah Ta'ala.

COLOUR IN THE WORDS

Money

Children

Health

Sabr

LESSON 12
HADHRAT AYYOOB
(alayhis salaam)

sickness	many years	dua
answered	healthy	blessed
spring	difficulty	strong

- Hadhrat Ayyoob (alayhis salaam) lived for many years with his wife, in **difficulty** and **sickness**.
- He still **remembered** Allah Ta'ala and **never ever complained**.
- He then **made dua** to Allah Ta'ala to **help him**.
- Allah Ta'ala was **very happy** with him
- Allah Ta'ala **answered his dua**.
- Allah Ta'ala caused a **spring of water** to gush from the ground and told Hadhrat Ayyoob (alayhis salaam) to **wash his body** with the water and **drink from it**.
- He did that and his **sickness disappeared**. He now became **strong** and **healthy** again.
- Allah Ta'ala then **returned** his **land**, **animals** and **money** to him.
- He and his wife were blessed with many **more beautiful children**.
- Allah Ta'ala was **very happy** with Hadhrat Ayyoob (alayhis salaam) because he did **not forget** Allah Ta'ala when he was in difficulty and sickness.

FILL IN THE BLANKS

Hadhrat Ayyoob (alayhis salaam) lived for many years with his wife, in _____ and sickness.

Allah Ta'ala answered his _____.

Allah Ta'ala then _____ his land, animals and money to him.

Allah Ta'ala was _____ with Hadhrat Ayyoob (alayhis salaam) because he did not _____ Allah Ta'ala when he was in difficulty and sickness.

Lessons from the life of Hadhrat Ayyoob *(alayhis salaam)*

- Make shukar (thank) to Allah Ta'ala for everything He has blessed us with.
- If we go through any difficulty, we must make sabr (be patient) and not complain.
- Make dua to Allah Ta'ala for help.
- Remember, after every difficulty, Allah Ta'ala will grant ease.

Activity: Class discussion

- Discuss all the things we need to make shukar for e.g., food, water, our parents, etc.
- Discuss some challenges people are faced with and how a Muslim should make Sabr e.g. sickness, death of a family member, etc.

LESSON 13

NABI MUHAMMAD ﷺ

- last
- best
- lucky
- ummah
- followers
- loves
- sallallahu alayhi wasallam

- Allah Ta'ala sent down many prophets to teach the people what is **right** and bring them back to **worshipping Allah Ta'ala**.
- The **last Nabi** that **Allah Ta'ala sent** was Nabi Muhammad (sallallahu alayhi wasallam).
- Whenever we hear the **name** of **Nabi Muhammad**, we should say **SALLALLAHU ALAYHI WASALLAM**.
- From all the prophets **Allah Ta'ala loves** Nabi Muhammad (sallallahu alayhi wasallam) **the most**.
- He is **the best** of prophets.
- We are very **lucky** because he is **OUR Nabi**.
- We are from the **Ummah** of **Nabi Muhammad (sallallahu alayhi wasallam)**. This means that we are **his followers**.
- We must **LOVE** our **Nabi Muhammad (sallallahu alayhi wasallam)** more than we love **anyone else**.

COLOUR IN

SALLALLAHU ALAYHI WASALLAM

LESSON 14

NABI MUHAMMAD
ﷺ

last	Abdullah	Aaminah
healthy	born	city
passed away	farm	Halimah

In the previous lesson we learnt that our Prophet's name is Muhammad (sallallahu alayhi wasallam) and he is the last of all the prophets. Now we are going to learn more about him.

- Nabi Muhammad (sallallahu alayhi wasallam) was **born** in **Makkah**.
- Nabi Muhammad's (sallallahu alayhi wasallam) **mother's** name was **Aaminah**.
- His **father's** name was **Abdullah**.
- His father passed away **before** he was **born**.
- His mother sent him to the **farm area/ countryside** to grow up **healthy** and **strong**.
- In the **country side**, he lived with **Hadhrat Halimah (radhiyallahu anha)** and **her family**.

FILL IN THE BLANKS

Nabi Muhammad (sallallahu alayhi wasallam) was born in _____.

His _____ name was Abdullah.

His father passed away before he was _____.

His mother's name was _____.

In the country side, he lived with _____ _____ and her family.

LESSON 15

NABI MUHAMMAD ﷺ

four years	loved	six years
Halimah	took care	Abu Taalib
grandfather	uncle	passed away

- Nabi Muhammad (sallallahu alayhi wasallam) stayed with Hadhrat Halimah (radhiyallahu anha) for four years.
- Thereafter he went back to Makkah to live with his mother.
- He lived with his mother for two years and then Hadhrat Aaminah passed away.
- Nabi Muhammad (sallallahu alayhi wasallam) was six years old when his mother passed away.
- Nabi Muhammad (sallallahu alayhi wasallam) now had no father and no mother.
- His grandfather, Abdul Muttalib, took care of him after his mother passed away.
- After two years his grandfather passed away.
- Nabi Muhammad (sallallahu alayhi wasallam) was eight years old at that time.
- Now his uncle whose name was Abu Taalib took care of him.
- Abu Taalib loved him very much.

FILL IN THE FAMILY TREE

LESSON 16

NABI MUHAMMAD ﷺ

grew up	fought	lie
truth	loved	helped
good	kind	old

Character of Nabi MUHAMMAD (sallallahu alayhi wasallam)

- Nabi Muhammad (sallallahu alayhi wasallam) **grew up** as a **very good child**.
- He was **very kind** to **everyone**.
- He **helped** the **old** and **weak people**.
- He **never** spoke **a lie**. He **always** spoke the **truth**.
- He never **fought** with anyone.
- Everyone **loved** him.

COLOUR IN USING THE SAME COLOURS SHOWN

36

LESSON 17

NABI MUHAMMAD ﷺ

think	angel	Jibraeel
Surah Alaq	cave	hira
young	forty	family

- Nabi Muhammad (sallallahu alayhi wasallam) **grew up** into a **young man**.
- When Nabi Muhammad (sallallahu alayhi wasallam) wanted some **quiet time**, he used to go to a **cave** in a **mountain** where he would sit and think of Allah.
- This cave is called the **Cave of Hira**.
- One day when he was in the cave of Hira, the **angel Jibraeel (alayhis salaam)** came to him with the **message** that Allah Ta'ala has chosen him as **His Nabi**.
- The angel Jibraeel read to Nabi Muhammad (sallallahu alayhi wasallam) the **first five Aayats** of **Surah Alaq**.
- Nabi Muhammad (sallallahu alayhi wasallam) was **forty years old** when Allah Ta'ala made him a **prophet**.
- Allah Ta'ala **commanded** Nabi Muhammad (sallallahu alayhi wasallam) to **call** the people of Makkah to **believe** in **one Allah Ta'ala**.
- Nabi Muhammad (sallallahu alayhi wasallam) began calling **his family**, **friends** and **people around him** to believe in Allah Ta'ala alone and **stop** worshipping idols.

- Most of them did not listen to him. Only a **few people accepted** his **message**.

COLOUR IN THE CAVE

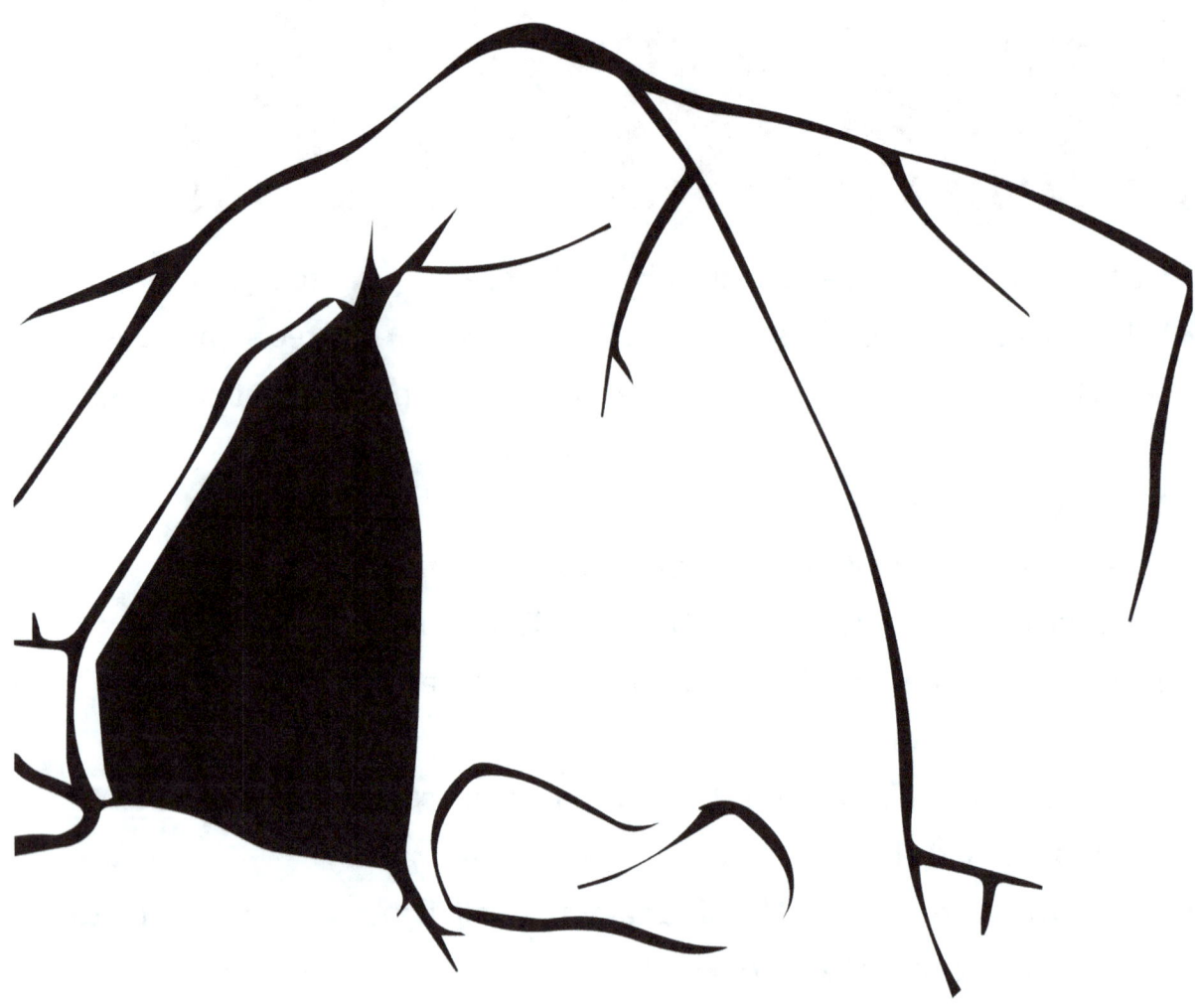